A Phenomenal Woman

Shining from Within

Andrea Brown

Copyright 2019 © Andrea Brown
ISBN 9781090403988

CONTENTS

ACKNOWLEDGEMENTS

Grandma Lesslie March 6th, 1904 to November 10th, 1991, Auntie Anne August 5th ,1947 to October 3rd ,2007 and Grandma Alice Heath December 4th ,1925 to September 20th, 2011.

Forever in my heart. I miss you.

GRANDMA LESSIE

I was born in Augusta Georgia. To understand Augusta, one must know a thing or two about the South. Especially the deep South during the civil war. According to summarized historical data found on Wikipedia; Augusta is located on the area along the river and long inhabited by varying cultures of indigenous peoples, who relied on the river for fish, water and transportation. Because of its location on the fall line, Augusta area was used as a place to cross the Savannah river. In 1735, two years after James Oglethorpe founded Savannah, he sent a detachment of troops to explore the upper Savannah River. He gave them an order to build a fort at the head of the navigable part of the river. The expedition was led by Noble Jones, who created a settlement as a first line of defense for coastal areas against potential Spanish or French invasion from the interior. Oglethorpe named the town in honor of Princess Augusta, the mother of King George III and the wife of Frederick, Prince of Wales. Oglethorpe visited Augusta in September 1739 on his return to Savannah from a perilous visit to Coweta Town, near present-day Phenix City, Alabama. There, he had met with a convention of 7,000 Native American warriors and concluded a peace treaty with them in their territories in northern and western Georgia. Augusta was the second state capital of Georgia from 1785 until 1795. Augusta developed rapidly as a market town as the Black Belt in the Piedmont was developed for cotton cultivation. Invention of the cotton gin made processing of short-staple cotton profitable, and this type of cotton was well-suited to the upland areas. Cotton plantations were worked by slave labor, with hundreds of thousands of slaves shipped from the Upper South to the Deep South in the domestic slave trade. Many of the slaves were brought from the Lowcountry, where their Gullah culture had developed on the large Sea Island cotton and rice plantations. The city experienced the Augusta Fire of 1916, which damaged 25 blocks of the town and many buildings of historical significance. As a major city in the area, Augusta was a center of activities during Reconstruction and after. In the mid-20th century, it was a site of civil rights demonstrations. In 1970 Charles Oatman, a mentally disabled teenager, was killed by his cellmates in an Augusta jail. A protest his death broke out in a riot involving 500 people, after six black men were killed by police, each found to have been shot in the back. The noted singer and entertainer James Brown were called in to help quell lingering tensions, which he succeeded in doing.

I must take you back on this journey. I was born in this city. The impact of slavery and poor state of African American in both civil and economic rights, hounded my ancestors. In me lies the blood of bitterness and pain from oppressive times. While on one hand we can point a finger at my absentee father, the other should point at the oppressive system that took the pride and responsibility of most men of color from raising their families. So yes, to this day I do not know my biological father. Its only by the grace of God that my mind is right. When you don't know your biological father, a hole inside of your soul lingers. And no matter what you do, or others tells you, the void remains. To understand the extend of this void, think of the questions, a person like me asks. Did he love me? What does he look like? Which part of me resembles him? And why did he leave me? Well that's just the start of this emotional void. In my case it was worse for my biological mother, lost custodial care of me and my siblings. To be clear it was not out of a court fight or anything like that, it was out of parental neglect. My great grand mother; took us in. She was the rock of our family. Lessie Bennett was a God-fearing matriarch. Church was the foundation of her social life. And I mean the foundation. She was in church and actively involved at that. Lessie was a member of the church choir. And that meant half her time was practicing for Sunday worship and preparing an agenda for her job. She loved to sing. Even at the house, she would've whipping up some eggs for breakfast and singing her favorite gospel tune. "He Lives" I would just stand by her side and watch her art and cooking skills. If we woke up and there was no sweet aroma of the coffee or eggs on a skillet, something was wrong. And no doubt about it. Talk about hard work! I get my work ethic from her. She was always working. Grandma enjoyed a good labor of the hand. She was not the type to settle for cramps falling off the table. Grandma was loved by many and members at the church. If she wasn't in the church choir, you'll easily find her in the committee. Especially the Food committee. She helped plan church events that involved catering for guests and members.

But don't let her kindness fool you. No one crossed my grandma. She did not allow any type of disrespect from anyone. Grandma Lessie had a dark skin complexion. But she always dyed her hair blue. That was her signature outfit. The lady with blue hair. Can you imagine easily identifiable my grandma was in a crowd? You couldn't miss her. And she loved her hair dyed blue. I loved that about her. The guts to live life with no fear of failure or intimidation. A strong woman indeed. I remember my friends were always afraid of her. But I had to assure them that she was warm, soft and fuzzy on the inside. When we played outside, grandma Lessie had rules. When the street lights came on, it was time to return to the house. There were repercussions for any violations or failure to do so. My fondest memories were her cooking. Oh Lord! Did we eat or what! She made sure our stomachs were full. She took pride in taking care of and raising us. And when it came to school work, education was important. I made sure to stayed out of trouble. Even though this was a tall order. I was one heck of a young girl. Its like trouble found me, or I found it. There was always a chance I was going to me something up. As a matter of fact, part of my rebellion was due to the internal pain and void of not having our mother and father around. It was not until later in my life that I realized, the condition was due to the idea of parental neglect. According to Psychology today;

Child neglect is defined as a type of maltreatment related to the failure to provide needed, age-appropriate care. Unlike physical and sexual abuse, neglect is usually typified by an ongoing pattern of inadequate care and is readily observed by individuals in close contact with the child. Once children are in school, personnel often notice indicators of child neglect such as poor hygiene, poor weight gain, inadequate medical care, or frequent absences from school. Professionals have defined four types of neglect: physical, emotional, educational, and medical. To readily admit that I struggled with the symptom of child neglect, would be an understatement. Since the issue with me was not abandonment but the feeling of being neglected by biological parents. I could not readily rectify why my parents were not the ones raising us. My siblings and I were in any physical, educational or medical neglect but emotional and psychological we were. This predisposition rendered our attention seeking behavior. And I believe that's why we longed for our parents. But instead of clearly articulating our struggles, we resorted to creating chaos every now and then just to get an attention to hopefully address the issue. But as you well know, grownups especially grandma; was set in her own ways. So, she was not going to discuss with us why our mother and father weren't there. Instead she took it upon herself to raise us and that she did. In so many better than most parents could've. I'm so grateful she never considered sending us or let the adoption care services take us to foster homes. I love and miss her so dearly. In addition to child neglect I learned that; *More children suffer from neglect in the United States than from physical and sexual abuse combined. The US Department of Health and Human Services found that in 2007 there were 794,000 victims of child maltreatment in the US, of those victims 59% were victims of neglect. Some researchers have proposed 5 different types of neglect: physical neglect, emotional neglect, medical neglect, mental health neglect, and educational neglect. States may code any maltreatment type that does not fall into one of the main categories—physical abuse, neglect, medical neglect, sexual abuse, and psychological or emotional maltreatment—as "other." – Psychology Today.*

Child neglect is an issue that rarely gets the same attention as physical and sexual abuse. Most researchers claim that the issue is very difficult to identify due to the various form's child neglect takes throughout a child's life. I can understand why this is so. Because on one hand, a child can be in loving home and well taken care of. A great education, meals, clothing and shelter, appear enough for nurturing. But when it comes to the issue of emotional and psychological stability, the assumption that all is well, no longer holds. We are humans and at some stage in our lives, we question our own history, family lineage and so forth. Internally even though young, we wanted to know about our parents just like anyone else would. But we were not old enough to understand any logical explanation so there lied the problem. When children experience neglect, they are likely to suffer from victimization. For example; In

2003, 47.3 percent of child victims were boys, and 50.7 percent of the victims were girls. The youngest children had the highest rate of victimization. The rate of child victimization of the age group of birth to 3 years was 16.5 per 1,000 children. The victimization rate of children in the age group of 4-7 years was 13.5 per 1,000 children. Nearly three-quarters of child victims (73.1 percent) ages birth to 3 years were neglected compared with 52.7 percent of victims ages 16 years and older. When I missed my foundational reconcilable point, "meeting my biological father," I felt victimized. In other words, "what was wrong with me?" That in of itself set me up to finding affirmation in others. After all the most important person in my life was absent. I acted out my frustrations. And I Knew my siblings experienced the same phenomenon. There were observable signs too, some days, I didn't care about my looks and then other I did. I later learned that it is normal to let it go when you feel neglected and victimized. In extreme cases I found out that common symptoms could include; being frequently absent from school, the value of money at a young age or the desire for it in the hope of attempting to buy love, medical care and eyesight, enough clothing, abuse of alcohol and drugs and lastly perpetual loneliness.

In some ways I developed a mild form of apathy. Its not that I was depressed but felt disconnected. Especially when I came around other kids who seemed to have a mother and father in the home. I would question myself as to why we didn't have the same. This created indifference in me. On one hand I wanted to get along with everyone but on the other, I didn't care too much for their opinions. Especially it violated my boundaries. I was not irrational or bizarre in character at all. I just didn't want anyone imputing their beliefs on me. And I think to a greater extend that came across as not caring. When people misunderstood me, it drove me inward. I closed and shut down. There were days when I disobeyed my grandma Lessie and would be gone from home every now and then. She cared for me and would not let me stray beyond correction. I could only but do so much of the rebellion. In school I did on occasion practice chronic truancy. If I didn't see the need to school, I could just not go. But that also happened during my rebellious cycles.

My grandma Lessie God bless her soul, made sure we stayed grounded throughout our emotional and spiritual struggles. She had a network of church members that helped her keep an eye on me. They would tell whenever we were spotted in violation and or our general whereabouts. So yes, we could only do so much. I credit her for teaching us how to work. She divided and distributed household chores equally and with consideration of ages. We were never a task beyond our abilities to accomplish. The challenge came when we decided not to complete it by her expectations. That when she'll broke loose. Grandma needed to be tough on us. She was aware of her aging and needed the assurance we could take care of ourselves in her absence. *And think this was part of my anger.* She was so loving and caring. For my parents not be there to take of us and for grandma to carry our burdens alone, was painful and stressful for her. I knew she would never admit to this fact. In some ways I blamed myself for her sickness whenever she fell ill. Getting older I thought that I didn't make things easier for her. I redirected that anger to myself especially when she was diagnosed with heart trouble and put on a low sodium diet. It was very painful and hard on me. I couldn't help but feel responsible. A fact I had to work and fight for a long time to forgive myself. Grandma was stubborn and set in her own ways. Back in the day, an African American woman took pride in her cooking. And if you knew anything about soul food, it will come natural to you that seasonings are a big part of the cooking experience. So, to ask grandma to forget about seasonings is like telling do not eat! Well you guessed it...she could not stop eating her food with seasonings.

She fought her illness with a vengeance. Till one day, the doctors insisted she be placed in a personal care home. To understand what my grandma was to experience, it's important to talk about long-term care. According to Wikipedia, *Long-term care can be provided formally or informally. Facilities that offer formal LTC services typically provide living accommodation for people who require on-site delivery of around-the-clock supervised care, including professional health services, personal care, and services such as meals, laundry and housekeeping. These facilities may go under various names, such as nursing home, personal care facility, residential continuing care facility, etc. and are operated by different providers.*

While the US government has been asked by the LTC (long-term care) industry not to bundle health, personal care, and services (e.g., meal, laundry, housekeeping) into large facilities, the government continues to approve that as the primary use of taxpayers' funds instead (e.g., new assisted living). Greater success has been achieved in areas such as supported housing which may still utilize older housing complexes or buildings or may have been part of new federal-state initiatives in the 2000s.

Long-term care provided formally in the home, also known as home health care, can incorporate a wide range of clinical services (e.g. nursing, drug therapy, physical therapy) and other activities such as physical construction (e.g. installing hydraulic lifts, renovating bathrooms and kitchens). These services are usually ordered by a physician or other professional. Depending on the country and nature of the health and social care system, some of the costs of these services may be covered by health insurance or long-term care insurance.

That meant that either the insurance or the government backed healthcare plans were to fund my grandma's stay at the health facility. Of course, to my immediate family, there was a temporary financial relief but to my grandma, the emotional disconnect from her daily routine and normality of living was a stretch. We were too young to take care of her in that condition. This took a toll on my life. Her granddaughter" Jeannie", lived a few blocks from us and agreed along with her daughter Alice Heath that grandma be placed in the personal care home. She needed 24-hour care services both medical and physical. We visited her while there, but grandma was never the same. That strong black woman was now hidden behind her ailing soul. The sorrow that engulfed my being was deep and dark. It took a lot of years to come out of it. To this day, it brings pains and sadness when I think about her pain. You must understand for person used to doing things her own way to depending on others, eating a restricted diet was too much on her.

I was 19 years old. That day November a Friday, I was sitting on the floor watching Television. I recall my grandma refusing to eat breakfast. A few nights and weeks had passed. She was not talking at all and if she did not that much. A few weeks earlier and leading up to this Friday, she kept asking for my sister and kept saying that I will miss her. I remember this one moment she told my younger sibling, "You'll all miss me. You don't do me right." I wondered why she kept saying that to us. But again, she was in so much pain and medication. So that Friday I knew something was not right. No breakfast and heard nothing much from her. So, television was a distraction for me. I wanted to ease my thoughts. My sister was in the bedroom with her. It was around 10 pm that night. My sister alerted me to her deteriorating condition. I came to the room. She asked for my other sibling. She hadn't seen her in a while.

Suddenly she gagged. As if something was in her throat. Visibly she looked like she had a stroke. We knew my middle sister needed to come sees her one last time. Things were not good at all. Panic and sadness surrounded our family. And for the first time, my only hope and stability in life was in question. But I could not let my mind cross that bridge. This was the last time, I saw and experienced my Great grandma Lessie. By the time my sister got home, it was too late. Our grandma was gone. She took it hard. We all did.

AUNTIE ANNE

When I think of a Phenomenal Woman, my Late Auntie Anne, comes to mind. She was born in 1947 and passed in 2007. She was a pillar and the glue that tied the family together. We were so close and shared everything about our history, life and education. My Auntie wanted the best for me especially returning to school. She always said she wanted me to be a nurse because whenever she got sick, I took great care of her. Thomas is my Auntie's only son. She was a very private person; quiet and shy. So, I got a lot of her ways. Our family was never the same again when we lost my Auntie in 2007. Her being gone and her Late mother (Madea) also. Left a void in my life. Our family had lost the two great matriarchs. I even got a pet for companionship. I needed to cope with the stresses in my life. It was not easy but God! Has a way with healing us. Words cannot fully express my gratitude to these two women being in my life and the role they each played. Dear God, I really miss my Auntie Anne. She knew her time was close. She requested that I visit her and talk like we always did. But because of my hectic schedule, I couldn't visit her on time. I truly believe she wanted to tell me what was going on with her health. I know she understood the cost of business ownership.

I had to be there most of the day; hardly any breaks between. I miss the stories we shared and the food we ate sometimes, late into the night. I will see in the Kingdom house.

MY EDUCATION

My early childhood education started in Augusta at W.S. Hornsby Elementary School. The school was named in honor of Walter Spurgeon Hornsby, Sr. (1882-1956). He was one of the founders of the Pilgrim Health and Life Insurance Company and the developer of Hornsby Subdivision. In 2007, W.S Hornsby Elementary School moved from Laney Walker Boulevard to Kentucky Avenue. Shortly after the relocation, the school was reclassified as a K-8. In 2009 it was merged with Wast Augusta Middle School and renamed W.S Hornsby 1-5th grade.

It was at this elementary school that my idea of education, social interaction with the world outside of my immediate family began to formulate. I remember the struggle to adopt and being an introvert, didn't help much. But again, given my circumstances, I was determined to put my best foot forward. Well I gained some friends even though I chose to observe rather than participate in many activities. At the time, discipline was acceptable and by that, I mean you would get a spanking for missed behavior. Even the principal would administer discipline in the event we were either disruptive or out of line. We were not spared.

My Grandma Lesslie, lived close to the school as a matter of fact, that the same home she lived till her retirement. As I got older to attend elementary school, she ensured my principal at school instilled discipline in me. She gave her permission to discipline me whenever I strayed. This move left me with no options but work hard in school and stay out of trouble. For some reason to this day I still remember my 4th grade teacher Mrs. Turner.

To let the truth be told I really did not like my teacher Mrs. Turner at all. In 5th grade I developed a sassy mouth. I hardly remember the name of my 5th grade teacher. By middle school I was feeling the puberty stage and that brought with it a complex of its own. I thought I had become my own woman! Yeah, I had opinions and a formulation of ideas to live by. I could dictate and charter my own path in life or so I thought. The one thing I kept consistency with was my education. That much I did. Homework and all. Middle school bound I was into a young lady stage and no one could not tell me nothing especially when my grades were good. all good. In 6th grade Mrs. Johnson my teacher was also a member of our church. She had a special connection with my grand mama Lesslie that way. So, she would visit our home and tell on me to my grandmother. Some of the things she said were true while others, a total misrepresentation of facts. This hurt me a lot for my grandma deserved truth and I hated false accusations. I just didn't stand a chance. She used to tell me, the only reason why she told on me was because of love and did not want me to lose my way in life. At the time I didn't want to hear all that. I felt as though she was lying to keep me in trouble with my Grandma, and my Grandma believed everything she said. So, I tried to stay away from her even in school, but it was hard because she was my homeroom teacher. Now Mrs. Burkeen our English teacher was loved by everyone in class. We couldn't wait to attend her teaching sessions. I remember vividly Mrs. Burkeen telling Mrs. Johnson to give me a break! Finally, someone stood up for me. It felt great! It was hard to leave Mrs. Burkeen's class. She was the best thing going for me at that time in school. Social studies were an okay subject, but I hated history classes. It was not until 8th grade that I knew to keep my grades up, I had to put an effort in my history classes. But as fate would have it, I saw it coming when Mrs. Johnson failed me in her class. I was embarrassed to say the list and that shaming I experienced left an emotional scar. An emotional scar is part of trauma. According to Wikipedia; *Psychological trauma is a type of damage to the mind that occurs as a result of a distressing event. Trauma is often the result of an overwhelming amount of stress that exceeds one's ability to cope, or integrate the emotions involved with that experience. Trauma may result from a single distressing experience or recurring events of being overwhelmed that can be precipitated in weeks, years, or even decades as the person struggles to cope with the immediate circumstances, eventually leading to serious, long-term negative consequences. Because trauma differs between individuals, according to their subjective experiences, people will react to similar traumatic events differently. In other words, not all people who experience a potentially traumatic event will become psychologically traumatized. This discrepancy in risk rate can be attributed to protective factors some individuals may have that enable them to cope with trauma; they are related to temperamental and environmental factors from among others. Some examples are mild exposure to stress early in life, resilience characteristics, and active seeking of help.* Not only did I fail Mrs. Johnson's class, I was left behind a grade. I saw my peers move to the next grade while I was held back. That damaged my confidence in school. I felt like I wasn't bright or intelligent enough. Even though I understood the reasons behind my failures in her class. On the second attempt, I passed the class.

In 8th grade, I went out of control and grandma was left without a choice. She decided it was better for me to move to New York City and live with my mother. That move terrified me. I understood the consequences of my actions. For the first I was truly being reprimanded for my behavior. New York City was way different than the southern small city of Augusta, Georgia. I knew I would be faced with different people who did not share the same background. Neighborhoods were going to be different than what I grew up knowing. Anxiety filled my life and thoughts. Moving to New York City, was frustrating to me because it was a different way of life and I was a scared young lady, just thinking, "Why I would not listen to my Grandma?" I had it easy in Augusta compared to New York City. Everyday I called collect to my grandmother and profusely apologized and begged for her forgiveness. I even told her it was so bad in New York, my mother had me sleep with a cat in the bed and I was afraid of cats. I told her I wanted to come back home to Augusta where I felt safe and loved. But that didn't help. 4 years had passed when my middle sister, auntie, and uncle came to visit. They had been informed by grandma about our plight. See my mother threatened us so bad...it was serious enough that our safety was on the line and so my grandma who practically raised was is no position to entertain that threat. She demanded we be returned to Augusta by any means necessary. So, the blessing in disguise was that I finally got my wish of returning home. Now one would ask why didn't you feel safe? After all you were living with your mother? Well only grown ups at the time had those answers. As far as I was concerned, I knew when things were not okay. All I could do is cry for help. But of course, I had created the situation that warranted being with my mother in New York City. My grandma felt sorry for having me go there too but I needed to learn my lesson. I told her that I was sorry and would do better. She heard my sincere apologies and she too, took responsibility for the situation. That was the best thing that could have happened to me by coming home to someone that loved me more than I loved myself at the time. Once I settled in, I showed gratitude by grounding myself in education, did my household chores and the change for the better could be seen by my family and friends. When I stayed with my mother for those few years, I had lapsed in education. She did not care about education the way my grandma did. So, there was a lot of catching up to do. My friend I call her my auntie Cynthia Harris, offered to tutor me so I could catch up. She was in college and her help was well worth it at the time. The late Mrs. Louise Harris Cynthia Harris mother made sure

I will have a bologna and cheese sandwich every time I came over for tutoring sessions.

I knew that I was on a short leash. I enjoyed talking on the phone during my breaks from homework. But even that had to be tamed. For I could not afford to lose the only hope I had of getting help with my education. Auntie Cynthia was no joke. She told me in advance that if I failed my exams again, she would no longer tutor me. That combined with the trouble I got myself into that landed me in New York City was too much of a risk to take. So, I made sure that I stayed on top of things this time around. Her family was so helpful. My cousin Nikki's auntie helped me in getting a job at the local VA hospital. On the days I didn't ride the bus to work, Cynthia, and her sister Sandra 'San' would pick me up and drop me off. I was so proud of myself. I could see progress once again. I made my own money and could buy my own life's necessities. I was able to give my sisters money when I had it and clothes after wearing Sky City and HL Green styles outfits and shoes for so long. It was a pleasure to buy what I could afford and change my outlook in life. These were some of my best years when I reminisce. This period was short lived when my grandma fell sick. We were forced to move in with my grandma's daughter. Everybody feared her. At least from the much I knew. I was only 16 years old at the time. So, I could not live independently or take care of my younger siblings alone. We lived about 30 minutes from my job at the VA. I was too scared to ask for rides from my grandmama for obvious reasons. I didn't want to get in her way. My grandma always let us play and even visit within reason, but my aunty was different altogether. We had to stay in her good graces and being in the house was mostly the only option we had. As an adolescent, there was always the worry that we could get involved with boys and get in trouble or even worse pregnant. The thing is we did but it was covertly done. There had to a balance between play time and school time. The issue was our freedom being restricted to such an extend that we felt, immobilized.

While grandma took ill, on many occasions I felt remorse for what I had done. I serially blamed myself for giving her a hard time. I wished I had done some of the things that I did. I felt the void in my life without her. She had become a mother to me. She was all I knew. I needed her voice more than ever. Even though my family meant well by taking us in and watched over us, we missed grandma immensely. If there was anything, I could do to get her health back in shape, you bet I would have. There was no denying she was the pillar of our family. To make matters worse, her level of understanding and wisdom, was needed by everyone too. So, it wasn't just me but all of us.

Deride Holmes, my best friend since middle school was always there for me during this time. Her family was well off financially compared to mine. But nonetheless we were best friends. Her father was adamant about school and good grades. He wanted her to pursue pos-secondary education. Sometimes I missed hanging out with her because she had to do more studies and extra prep-work for college. At that time, it appeared as though suggestively; we would ruin Deride's academic ambitions. This in some ways made me a little jealous. I too wanted a father who could fight for my well-being like that. Over the years we grew older and apart. Eventually Deride moved to Atlanta, joined Kennesaw University and pursued her undergrad. As I got older, I began to process rejection as being taken advantage of. Many of the people I was surrounded by, only needed me for what I could give and not who I was. Eventually I developed boundaries for good or for worse. I chose to be close to people who valued education and stayed the narrow path of less pleasure and more focused on success. It was not easy for I love people and making friends, but life's experiences had painted a different picture for me. Most of my childhood friends went to do things in life that had nothing to do with education, business or successful ventures. But a few chose the right path of education. I chose to do the same. I enrolled in college to study accountancy. Business always fascinated me, so it was easier to study something I really enjoyed. But that's how my affinity to helping and nurturing young minds came to be. I volunteered in school systems with the CSRA, in both Georgia and South Carolina and worked as a teacher's aid in some instances while in others mentored young students.

My love life is worth reckoning with. To help you understand, I've always had a crush or a thing for brown skinned males. Now maybe because opposites attract; I do not know. But that is part of my psychological make up when it comes to attraction. This part of my life is a challenge all together. For on one hand I know its an attractive attribute to desire what I want but on the other, how can one control and get what they want? See for humans, we have a will and a right to pursue our desires but on the flip side it takes two to tango. This affinity for brown skinned males, landed me in a relational regret. I remember my first crush. He's name was Brady. He was everything I thought I ever wanted. He was not brown skinned either. When he made a move, I played the shy, reserved as a quiet girl. I guess I got that wrong. For the next thing I knew, another woman, got him before I sealed the deal. This is how painful it was, I saw them embrace in the park. But they did not see me. Upon inquiry, I was told that he said I was too reserved. In other words, I moved too slow. I guess it wasn't meant to be. But to tell you the truth, it hurt beyond words. I was leveled down emotionally. I turned my focus to doing business, work and make money. Now that I could control.

I'm an introvert. According to Wikipedia -Introversion is the state of being predominantly interested in one's own mental self. Introverts are typically perceived as more reserved or reflective. Some popular psychologists have characterized introverts as people whose energy tends to expand through reflection and dwindle during interaction.

Introverts often take pleasure in solitary activities such as reading, writing, using computers, hiking, or fishing. The archetypal artist, writer, sculptor, scientist, engineer, composer, and inventor are all highly introverted. An introvert is likely to enjoy time spent alone and find less reward in time spent with large groups of people, though they may enjoy interactions with close friends. Trust is usually an issue of significance: a virtue of utmost importance to introverts is choosing a worthy companion. They prefer to concentrate on a single activity at a time and like to observe situations before they participate, especially observed in developing children and adolescents. They are more analytical before speaking. Introverts are easily overwhelmed by too much stimulation from social gatherings and engagement, introversion having even been defined by some in terms of a preference for a quiet, more minimally stimulating external environment.

Mistaking introversion for shyness is a common error. Introversion is a preference, while shyness stems from distress. Introverts prefer solitary to social activities, but do not necessarily fear social encounters like shy people do. Western culture misjudges the capabilities of introverted people, leading to a waste of talent, energy and happiness. Our society is biased against introverts, and that, with people being taught from childhood that to be sociable is to be happy, introversion is now considered "somewhere between a disappointment and pathology".

African American Lived Experiences and Challenges to Post-Secondary Education.

African American students face many hindrances to achieving their dream for post-secondary education. To begin with our living conditions are or at below poverty. Think about the neighborhoods with a high rate of violent crimes and gang activities, lack of parental involvement in their education, and distractions from academics by the over usage of social media. These obstacles inhibit the probability of African American students from prioritizing education. It starts early and from home. From my childhood lived experiences, the more involved my family was in my education, raised my expectation to succeed. and partly because I did not want to let them down but also because I needed to prove I was intelligent. In the earlier chapter I eluded to the fact that it took a community's involvement in my overall upbringing and being held accountable for my actions whether good or bad. But with the advancement in technology, our children are more likely to indulge in social media than study and read books to gain knowledge. And in turn limits the chances for post-secondary success, making it more difficult for African American students to pursue higher education. For example, poor or failing grades in high school could also increase the dropout rate among African American students. Imagine that Low ACT scores and grade point averages (GPA), limits the chances for post-secondary education for our children. In my doctoral research, I focused on the lived experiences of African American students and the impact these experiences have on their post-secondary education. I emphasize post-secondary education because, without having a clear goal in mind, higher education stays as a dream. Part of the challenge with our youth is that parents and even teachers do not emphasize graduation from high school to college as being important and vital for success. Students therefore are likely to consider high school graduation as being significant enough when it's just the first step. Better economical opportunities are possible with a higher or post-secondary education than without.

It is not known how academically disengaged African American students describe their lived experiences and challenges to post-secondary success and what they recommend as solutions to overcoming those lived experiences and challenges; I decided to research this phenomenon through; Focus groups, Surveys and Interviews. It is not known how academically disengaged African American high school students describe their lived experiences and challenges to post-secondary success and what they recommend as solutions to overcoming those lived experiences and challenges. Academic disengagement happens when students are no longer motivated in school, and can be indicated by underachievement, poor attendance, and receiving more frequent disciplinary action. According to the U.S. Department of Education, in 2009 there were around eight million African American students in the United States public school system. Almost 70% of African American students do not graduate from a four-year institution within six years of completing high school, which means that over 5.5 million of those students will likely not complete a college degree (Kim & Hargrove, 2013).

"African American students are less likely to succeed in college because the high schools they attend do not properly prepare them" (Bryant, 2015, pg. 15). Continued work in this field is essential to help shape federal, state, and local policies that improve education quality for African American students (Bryant, 2015). Young Black males have traditionally been cautious when it comes to trust. In American society in general, and specifically in educational institutions, Black males have consistently confronted negative cultural and academic stereotypes that paint them as being intellectually inferior (Steele, 1997). In her study research, Rhonda Tsoi-A-Fatt Bryant (2015), African American students are less likely to succeed in college because the high schools they attend do not properly prepare them. In addition, Bryant emphasizes the need for continued work in this field as being essential to helping shape federal, state, and local policies that improve education quality for African American students. College readiness is the combination of core academic knowledge, skills, and habits that youth need to be successful in a post-secondary setting without remedial coursework or training (Lombardi, Seburn, & Conley, 2011). Comparative data and intervention techniques from other countries with higher instances of Black males graduating high school could be helpful in deciding upon appropriate intervention strategies for schools in America (Conley 2011). Readiness for post-secondary education. African American high school students rely on several important sources of support in preparation for post-secondary enrollment and success including family support, peer advice, and test preparation (Baber, 2014). Immediate family and a sense of family history was shown to be critical in prioritizing education and college aspirations from an early age (Baber, 2014). Older peers who were further along in their college careers serve as valuable sources of honest information and advice for how to best utilize college resources for high school students (Baber, 2014).

A commonly given explanation for this disparity is that African American high school students are academically disengaged. Students who have access to college-level academics in high school are more likely to seek and succeed in higher education (McGee, 2013; Roderick, Coca, & Nagaoka, 2011). African American high school students do not expect to meet the minimum qualifications for post-secondary education. However, critical race research has argued that disengagement often stems from the gendered racism challenges that African American male students face because of their "blackmaleness" (James &Lewis, 2014; Wood, 2014). These challenges include, but are not limited to, being stereotyped (e.g., being aggressive or better suited for sports than academics), being questioned or dismissed intellectually, being intensively surveyed on school campuses, and experiencing low faculty or teacher expectations (Brooms, 2018). These types of challenges that African American high school students face are important to explore further from the student's perspective because they complicate the common notion that African American males are simply not interested in or are disengaged from higher education (Wood, 2014).

Thus, arguing that disengaged African American high school students would not be interested in post-secondary success is an oversimplification of a complex issue that involves both individual and structural-level issues. Moreover, it would be improper to label a student as wholly engaged or disengaged (Hancock & Zubrick, 2015). The issue of academic disengagement among African American high school students, then, is indeed multifaceted and warrants further exploration.

Despite their academic engagement and achievement, African American male students still reported contending with a lack of mentorship and community support, microaggressions from White students and teachers, and other problems as barriers to their academic success (Warren, 2016). However, research studies on the academically disengaged African American high school students has not been fully studied.

The Single Black Woman Challenge

According to an article published by Chicago Tribune and written by columnist Darrel Rockett, *Researchers argue in a 2015 study that a racial gap in marriage emerged in the 1960s, when black marriage rates started to decline, first slowly then steeply. Recent data suggest that, at all ages, black Americans have lower marriage rates than other racial and ethnic groups. Based on U.S. Census Bureau data from 2008 to 2012, less than two-thirds of black women were married by their early 40s, compared with almost nine out of 10 white and Asian/Pacific Islander women and more than eight in 10 Hispanic women.*

In her findings many women over the age of 40 years admit to knowing that the challenge to dating marriage exists partly due to knowledge that black women in this age group know what they want in a relationship. There is also an acknowledgment to the reality that other races, date with a purpose. Meaning they have a marriage, similar goals and desires in life. Which in turn helps them cope with challenges as they rise within their relationship. And as women get older love and stability becomes more important than money or material gain. The looking Superman syndrome diminishes with age. Men within this age bracket especially black men, from the same article indicate that dating does not work because women play mind games.

Now whether there exists truth in this phenomenon or not, the bottom line is that relationships are a challenge and more so to women or color. The reason I wrote this chapter is to encourage women of color like myself to focus on the good; the contributions we make in our society, starting with the very communities we live in. No matter what happens with relationships, there is one issue we all must deal with...Children! Babies! We keep making them. And guess what someone must nurture them. So, whenever we see a young man out of line or a young woman pregnant, we must not turn or look the other way. This is us. Yes, you and me. We bring them to this world and whether we like it or not, we owe them a good home, education and nurture. Failure to do so, only adds to the frustration. We must also hold accountable men that father our children. The day and age where fathers just walk away from their children has passed. The sad truth is we should not allow young children to experience fatherlessness. I'm trying advocate for marriage here. But parental responsibilities. It more than just paying child support. It about being there. As an educational volunteer, mentor and a doctoral student in education; all children deserve a loving home, proper nutrition and care before education. And without our women coming together and addressing the issue of childcare and welfare without shifting that responsibility to school systems, not much can be done by teachers.

One of my favorite saying, 'it takes a village to raise a child,' is true then and now. No adult with a child is off the hook from his or her parental responsibility. This was the hardest part of my life. If grandma was not in my life, I do not know where I would be. She became my father and my mother. But most importantly, she took on the burden of doing both. She was also wise enough to allow the community to help her raise me. Starting from her church members, neighbors and my teachers. She never stood in the way. Did not let me manipulate or lie about my whereabouts. She held me responsible and the community supported her. The key thing here is that she was active in my life. And as I stated earlier, I saw a major difference in my education when I moved away from her home. While in New York City, education was not emphasized neither was it a priority. To this day that move affected me. Your children, our children can tell the difference. They may not readily admit it to you but disciplining and holding them accountable is very appreciated. And young students will admit that they need discipline from their parents and care takers. Especially as they mature. They need your guidance always!

The issue of singleness among our women is that we keep hoping as in the movies that Mr. Right is going to just show up. So, we don't work hard with what we have. Listen to me, everything is work. By the time Mr. Right shows up, there is life to be lived. And if you have children, raising is a priority. My grandma gave me the strength and wisdom to becoming a phenomenal woman. To be phenomenal woman, you must deal with life's issue head on. You must bounce back from temporary setbacks, you must climb the ladder when others are coming down. You must negotiate your needs and desires without fear of rejection. And when the dust settles, pat yourself on the shoulders for the hard-work if no one cheers you on.

STUDIES

Introversion

Extraversion and introversion

Author: Wikipedia contributors

Publisher: Wikipedia, The Free Encyclopedia.

Permanent link:

https://en.wikipedia.org/w/index.php?title=Extraversion_and
_introversion&oldid=886454530

Primary contributors: Revision history statistics

Page Version ID: 886454530

Augusta, Georgia

Author: Wikipedia contributors

Publisher: Wikipedia, The Free Encyclopedia.

Permanent link:

https://en.wikipedia.org/w/index.php?title=Augusta,_Georgia
&oldid=886899672

Primary contributors: Revision history statistics

Page Version ID: 886899672

Long-term Care

Author: Wikipedia contributors

Publisher: Wikipedia, The Free Encyclopedia.

Permanent link:

https://en.wikipedia.org/w/index.php?title=Long-term_care&oldid=884769013

Primary contributors: Revision history statistics

Page Version ID: 884769013

Dating Black and Over 40

Chicago Tribune-Feb 15, 2018
https://www.chicagotribune.com/lifestyles/ct-life-dating-while-black-over-40-2018-story.html

Excerpts from my Doctoral Research

African American male students experience significant challenges in school. On average, are less likely to succeed compared to other races and have the lowest persistence rates (Adelman, 2005). African American males lag on almost every indicator of academic achievement (Esters & Mosby, 2007). There are several reasons behind these and originated from racial inequalities in race, social class, chronic unemployment and a lack of role models (Gavins, 2009). For academic success, schools must be equipped with a well-qualified and competent teaching staff and evidence suggests that the quality of teaching, students receive is the most important in-school factor affecting their achievement (Thompson, Warren, Foy, & Dickerson, 2008). Low-income struggles outside of school is not the only factor contributing to academic disengagement and challenges to post-secondary education African American male high school students. Critical aspects of teacher quality include; high-level and challenging courses, high expectations from teachers and positive relationships between teachers and students. A major difference between schools that serve high proportions of African American students and those that do not is the number of well-qualified, highly experienced teachers (Flores, 2007). African American students are four times more likely than white students to attend a school where 80 percent or fewer teachers are certified (U.S. Department of Education, 2014b). Four percent of African American students attend a school where more than 20 percent of teachers are in their first teaching year, as compared to only one percent of white students (United States Department of Education, 2014b).

African American males especially have historically had low rates of post-secondary enrollment, especially when compared to that of other races, ethnicities, and genders (Kim & Hargrove, 2013). More research is needed to study this phenomenon. (Bartz, 2016) accredited this low rate of post-secondary success to several institutional, socioeconomic, racial, and historical circumstances that directly affect African American male students' engagement in education. According to research on college and career planning, schools' counselors can be highly effective advocates, helping students identify their best options based on their potential and goals (Ward, 2006). High school counselors are critical in assessing, evaluating and advising students. Counselors must have high expectations for all students and work collaboratively to ensure their success (Bryan, Holcomb-McCoy, Moore-

Thomas, & Day-Vines, 2009; Reid & Moore, 2008). In their roles as advocates, school counselors should work with low-income African American students and their families to address marginality, culture, and power relationships that limit college preparedness (Holcomb-McCoy, 2010).

"Trust Me, You Are Going to College": How Trust Influences Academic Achievement in Black Males by Stuart Rhoden (2015), in the past few decades, a significant shift has occurred in scholarship surrounding Black males from deficit models to scholarship focused on positive strength-based assets of Black male students. Darling-Hammond (2007), Ladson-Billings (2006) and Noguera (2008) have articulated how notions of inferiority found in earlier literature focusing on the study of Black males in education fixated on students' deficiencies rather than their positive achievements. The prevailing belief is that deficit-based thinking has hampered policymakers, educators and in many ways, Black males themselves, into believing their deficits were too significant to overcome and most importantly said criticisms were accurate. Therefore, the belief is that a self-fulfilling prophecy helped reinforce in many young Black male students that there was little hope of attaining positive academic achievement. This perspective, does not provide researched data based or the methodology on how Black males, describe their experiences and challenges to post-secondary education. Self-fulfilling prophesy is too vague of an assumption without tangible data collected from a sample of African American male high school students.

According to Steel (1997), in order to create more positive educational outcomes, it is critical to examine why some young Black males succeed in the face of adversity while many of their peers do not. Young Black males have traditionally been cautious when it comes to trust. In American society in general, and specifically in educational institutions, Black males have consistently confronted negative cultural and academic stereotypes that paint them as being intellectually inferior. This study examined the lives of Black males from their own perspective, as well as the perspective of their high school administrator, and college counselor. To obtain the perspective of the students themselves, ten semi-structured interviews were conducted with graduates of the Class of 2011 from Du Bois Charter High School who were in their second year of college. Du Bois High School was a predominantly Black, all-male charter school in a major urban city in the Mid-Atlantic. The interviews focused primarily on participants' background experiences (both growing up as well as their high school experiences) while at Du Bois Charter as well as their college academic environment. This research study was limited to a charter school. While student sample came from the same neighborhood and similar socioeconomic conditions, a decision to leave public school systems for a private charter school had been made. It's also clear that the sample of students in this research study came from home backgrounds where parents or guardians played an active role in their academic life. We know so because the decision to leave public schools was based on academic performance and post-secondary success. One of the things proponents of charter schools contend separates them from their neighborhood public schools is a that charter schools may have fewer bureaucratic obstacles, they have a greater chance of assessing students' academic needs, and they quickly respond more specifically and culturally appropriate than the larger district. While the data from Du Bois Charter does not represent the totality of educational experiences of all Black males in public education in this country, there are some recommendations one can draw from their stories. Research focusing on such a small sample size cannot definitively speak to the multitude of circumstances Black male students encounter in public education, it can suggest a few recommendations.

Academic Disengagement

Academic disengagement refers to when students are no longer motivated in school, and can be indicated by academic underachievement, poor attendance, and receiving more frequent disciplinary action (Henry et al., 2015). Though academically disengaged African American male High school students may not perform well in high school, they may still have post-secondary aspirations which are affected by their academic disengagement in high school (Wood, 2014). School counselors play a crucial role in post-secondary readiness for African American male High school students. Much like their teachers, High school counselor's training, high expectations, and authentic relationships are essential and necessary in High school. Academic disengagement among African American male High school students is due in part to the reality that they can be steered toward less rigorous post-secondary options by counselors. Especially, if counselors are skeptical about their success to post-secondary education (Long et al.,2009). Academic disengagement can also be attributed to a lack of planning in courses beyond the minimum required for graduation and post-secondary success by academic counselors to African American male High school students (Long et al.,2009; Reid & Moore, 2008; Ward 2006). Without proper guidance, African American male High school students often don't realize that by not taking rigorous High school courses hurts their college prospects (Reid & Moore, 2008; Welton & Martinez, 2014).

According to a research study; Preparation for African American Students: Gaps in the High School Educational Experience by Rhonda Tsoi-A-Fatt Bryant (2015), College readiness is the combination of core academic knowledge, skills, and habits that youth need to be successful in a postsecondary setting without remedial coursework or training (Lombardi, Seburn, & Conley, 2011). College and career readiness aren't solely determined by the courses one takes; students must also understand college culture, have strong study habits, and know how to access supports (Lombardi et al., 2011). The four elements of college readiness are cognitive strategies, content knowledge, academic behaviors, and contextual skills and awareness (Conley, 2010). Cognitive strategies

According to Tsoi-A- Byrant (2015), 'African American students are less likely to succeed in college because the high schools they attend do not properly prepare them. Continued work in this field is essential to help shape federal, state, and local policies that improve education quality for African American students. It is not known how academically disengaged African American male high school students describe their lived experiences to post-secondary success and what they recommend as solutions to overcome those experiences. Henry et al. (2015) connected academic disengagement to academic underachievement as an early warning risk factor for later negative consequences such as dropping out and stated that many African American males especially were at risk for academic disengagement, underachievement, and ultimately dropping out. Academic disengagement can be evidenced by a lack of desire to engage in class, with peers, or outside the classroom (Wood, 2014). Academic success is negatively affected by academic disengagement (Wood, 2014).

Wood (2014) conducted a study on engagement of African American males in community college and found that many students had difficulty with engaging in class. This academic disengagement could be seen in a refusal to participate in class activities and discussion, ask questions, or utilize office hours. Students identified a sense of apprehension in engaging in these activities but were not always able to identify their reasons for their apprehension. Wood (2014) found that they feared being perceived as unintelligent and inferior, and of being dismissed or otherwise marginalized. He also found that students felt that they were unfocused, shy, or apprehensive of higher expectations. Nevertheless, Wood attributed a large part of academic disengagement and disidentification to be a way to cope with being racially stereotyped in academic environments, which is further exacerbated by a stereotyped perception of African American males who avoid seeking help.

Henry et al. (2015) found that by using students' school records as an indicator of academic disengagement, students at risk for dropping out and later problem behaviors could be identified. A failure to complete and graduate from high school can lead to not only a failure to achieve post-secondary success, but also long-term negative consequences (Henry et al., 2015). The researchers stated that there was still a need for more research on academic disengagement. According a research study by Bryssa Koppie (2017) The Black Male Achievement Gap: Strategies for Intervention, the strength of the study involved student participants from many age groups, geographic locations and life experiences. Qualitative interviews in the Bell (2014) and Welch (2013) articles added a deeper understanding of the ways in which Black students feel they are included and excluded in school. The inclusion of administrators as research participants in the Lee-Currie (2013) study brought a unique intervention to the forefront of the systematic review. However, the limitations of the study were that the articles' scope of research was overall small. All studies used in the review were conducted in one school, city or region within the United States. Another limitation to the study was that most of the examined research focused on the way that school did not equitably support Black male students and did not consider other environmental factors like neighborhood crime, family of origin, poverty, etc

The areas for future research, According to Bryssa Koppie (2017), should focus on the Black male high school graduation rates and successful interventions to increase graduation rates across the country. Additionally, familial communication patterns and support should be included in future research as positive familial interactions is correlated to increased psychological well-being for Black males; which, in turn, influences their academic success (Rowley & Bowman, 2009). Finally, comparative data and intervention techniques from other countries with higher instances of Black males graduating high school could be helpful in deciding upon appropriate intervention strategies for schools in America.

Readiness for post-secondary education

African American male High school students rely on several important sources of support in preparation for post-secondary enrollment and success including family support, peer advice, and test preparation (Baber, 2014). Immediate family and a sense of family history was shown to be critical in prioritizing education and college aspirations from an early age (Baber, 2014). Older peers who were further along in their college careers serve as valuable sources of honest information and advice for how to best utilize college resources for high school students (Baber, 2014). High stakes testing that determines college readiness have proved to be essential in determining college readiness, although a balance of nontraditional and traditional cultural capital is necessary for students to succeed in graduating with higher education degrees (Baber, 2014).

The recommended student-to-counselor ratio is 250-to-1 (Bemak, Chi-Ying, Siroskey-Sabdo, 2005). However, the current average in the United States is 471-to-1 (American School Counselor Association, 2013). An astounding 20 percent of high schools have no school counselor at all (US Department of Education, 2014a). Smaller and more affluent schools tend to have smaller counselor-to-student ratios and more college focus (Bryan et al., 2009; Holland & Farmer-Hinton, 2009).

Common challenges in high school for African American males

Negative Stereotypes.

Stereotypical threats, marginalization, and a lack of significant role models are major factors in the educational experiences of African American males (Scott & Rodriguez, 2014). Teachers often perpetrate negative beliefs about African American male students and leverage their power and privilege in the classroom to the detriment of African American male students (Scott & Rodriguez, 2014). Moon and Singh stated that African American males were negatively perceived by teachers and administrators, and that students often conform to these negative stereotypes which limit success in school. A feeling of neglect from teachers and peers made it especially difficult for African American male students to invest the time and energy necessary to achieve academic success. (Moon & Singh 2015). It was also challenging for

African American males to exhibit the behaviors associated with being a good student and "staying out of trouble" (Moon & Singh, 2015). This belief has had negative effects on African American students and is correlated with low teacher expectations and disproportionate rates of punishment which eventually can lead to disengagement (Puchner & Markowitz, 2015).

As a result, African American male students are often overrepresented in special education courses, regardless of whether they have been formally diagnosed with a learning disability, have different learning needs that the teacher does not meet, or needs psychological testing to address a mental health issue that has been neglected. These factors have a detrimental effect on engagement and learning. In, "Banks, 2017," many African American male students regarded their disability labels as unnecessary burdens that, along with their race, gender, and socioeconomic statuses, contributed to different and lowered expectations from teachers and peers, increased pressures to prove their intellectual ability, and increased need to develop coping strategies for the expectations placed upon them (Banks, 2017). Labeling African American male students as having learning disabilities also isolates and segregates them into separate classrooms away from general education classrooms while placing them under more restrictions, reinforcing the racial and gender biases that influence African American male's school experiences (Banks, 2017).

Gender Bias.

Voyer & Voyer (2014) discussed the existence of a "female advantage" in schools across most course subjects, wherein females generally perform better in academics than males. Ezeala-Harrison (2014) suggested that this may partially be due to gender differences in faculty interactions, which highlight the fact that black females generally benefit much more from faculty interaction and mentorship than black males, who usually employ a more independent approach to their academics.

Single sex education has also been suggested as a potential alternative to traditional educational settings in order to address the negative effects female bias on African American male students (Bowe, Desjardins, Clarkson & Lawrenz, 2017). One study on single sex classrooms for black male students emphasized the importance of developing trusting relationships between teachers and students and the need for teachers to show care for and investment in students in order to positively shape students' experiences (Flennaugh, 2017).

Stereotype threat

Stereotypes associated with black males can have a considerable effect on their studies. In 2016, Tyler, Thompson, Gay, Burns, Lloyd, and Fisher, conducted a study wherein African American males internalized the negative stereotypes of them being lazy, vicious, criminal, and unintelligent. These study participants were more likely to self-handicap when it came to school and thus performed worse academically the more that they internalized these notions. This phenomenon is due to "stereotype threat," which Tomasetto and Appoloni (2013) defined as the anxiety that arises when a stigmatized individual is at risk of failing and ultimately proving the stereotype to be correct. This study showed that it has tangible, measurable effects on likelihood of student success. Discrimination based on social status, trauma associated with excessive punishment, and negative stereotypes based on race and gendered can have deleterious effects on African American male identity, self-actualization, and perceptions of their masculinity, which put them at greater risk of developing mental health issues and contribute to their increased reluctance to seek out and utilize mental health and counseling services (Evans, Hemmings, Burkhalter & Lacy, 2015).

Stereotype threat theory has also been used in research to investigate high-achieving African American student perceptions of achievement. Research suggests that African American students often feel an intense pressure to disprove the stereotype of being naturally unintelligent, which has emotionally debilitating effects on students themselves (Wasserberg, 2017). Students in these circumstances often believe that their education is being focused on preparation for standardized testing. They reported increased feelings of anxiety related to testing and a concern with how they would perform in relation to the stereotypes that others place upon them (Wasserberg, 2017). Johnson-Ahorlu (2013) corroborated these effects in African American undergraduate students, who perceived stereotypes and stereotype threat to be one of the major barriers to their collegiate success. Stereotype threat was shown to distract students, reduce memory capacity, and overall slow students' progress to degree completion. The loss of confidence that results from stereotype threat can inhibit the way students engage in classroom activities, small groups, problem solving, and other methods of classroom participation, which can additionally impact students' overall progress toward academic success (Grant, Crompton & Ford, 2015).

Negative stereotypes of black men are considerable barriers to them becoming teachers and being able to set positive role models for future students (Ononuju, 2016). This can result in black male educators in being overlooked for their ability to connect with black male students due to them not meeting mainstream expectations of what an educator should look like (Ononuju, 2016).

Lack of role models

In, "Scott, Taylor & Palmer," study to challenge the negative representations of African American males, students that were interviewed advocated a need for mentorship and positive images and representations of black males in society (Scott, Taylor & Palmer, 2013). Positive representations and inspiring messages aimed at African American male students have been essential to efforts by educators to address and subvert the stereotypes and stereotype threat, and consequently engage black males in school increase the level of engagement by African American males in schools (Johnson, 2015).

Fathers play a particularly critical role in being role models for students, employing spiritually-grounded disciplinarian parenting styles while providing financial stability for the family (Odom & McNeese, 2014).

Positive role models and trusting relationships with teachers and administrators are an integral aspect of African American male students' willingness to engage and possess a positive perception of school (Ononuju, 2016). Ononuju (2016) stressed the importance of having African American male administrators and faculty at schools that are majority African American so that that African American male students can have access to positive role models to the male students in the academic setting. According to Ononuju (2016), additional importance of "indigenous" black teachers, where "indigenous" referred to a person's connection to the community from birth to their retirement and beyond.

Excessive punishment

Negative stereotypes of African American males contribute significantly to the disproportionate ratio of disciplinary referrals of African American male students. Martin, Sharp-Grier, and Smith (2016) stated that African American students, along with Native Americans, were referred for discipline at much higher levels than any other group within the academic setting. African American males were additionally more likely to receive punishment than females. This finding is validated in Simmons-Reed, and Cartledge (2014) research, that revealed that disproportionate punishment received by African American males has negative effects on larger society due to a lack of cultural awareness. The study also recommends reassessment of the school resource officer, having on-site mentoring programs, and developing a plan to improve teacher-student relations as possible solutions to limit disproportionate punishment. Gagnon, Gurel, and Barber (2017) also stated similar findings when researching the disproportionate discipline of African American males in school.

Disproportionate punishment of African American males was exacerbated by zero-tolerance policies originating in the 1970s, which were meant to cut down on suspension rates however this policy had the opposite effect, doubling the racial-ethnic gap in school suspension rates. It created a hostile and alienating school environment and caused African

Americans students to be disciplined at rates that far exceeded their representation in schools (Blake, Gregory, James & Hasan, 2016).

Furthermore, African American men are overrepresented in prisons, and face an extremely high one in three chance of being incarcerated in their lifetimes, the highest likelihood out of any other demographic group (Aguilar, 2015). Spending on prisons and the rate of incarcerations has significantly surpassed spending on education in the United States since the 1980s despite the overall decreasing rates of crime, which shows the racially targeted effects of mass incarceration (Aguilar, 2015). Being convicted of drug-related offenses can even hurt a student's chances of receiving financial aid for school (Aguilar, 2015). Additionally, black male teachers reported feeling an increased pressure to enforce authoritarian discipline and handle student misconduct of black male students (Brockenbrough, 2014). The teachers believed that this was due to both the expectation that adult black men were "scary" and that black men were naturally disciplinarian (Brockenbrough, 2014). They come to perceive school as a place that ignores their aspirations and abilities, fails to recognize their experiences, and restricts their identity (Dancy II, 2014).

Socioeconomic challenges.

Family and community wealth can be major predictors of academic achievement. Schools are better-funded and provide greater access to enrichment activities in high property tax locations. The location and economic status of a school district can impact the quality of a child's nutrition, family structure, peer influence, and the rate of parental incarceration (Bartz, 2016). Simmons (2013) found that the economic status and background of a student's family was very influential to their likelihood of college retention through graduation. Berliner (2013) argued that income inequality was the primary factor in the failure of many school reform measures in the past, and thus eliminating income inequality would go farther in improving school performance than additional teacher training.

Often, African American males must take on additional family obligations while being a student. Thus, being a student is not always their primary focus. These obligations and responsibilities influence their academic lives. In addition to school requirements, these students must navigate issues including having families that are struggling financially and relocating often, obligations to contribute financially, family problems, and the appeal of selling drugs despite knowing risks of death or prison (Moon & Singh, 2015).

Threats to physical safety are the most apparent obstacles to growing up in poverty. Prince, Epstein, Nurius, King, Gorman-Smith, and Henry (2016) showed that African American male adolescents living in low income neighborhoods expected to encounter threats to their safety within five years, and that they believed in their likelihood of premature death. Poor neighborhoods experience greater presence of militarized police, who racially target African American youth and increase the likelihood of incarceration (Desai & Abeita, 2017). These issues cause African American youth to be more aware and conscious of their movements within those areas and regard their neighborhoods as major obstacles to education (Brooms, 2015). In a study by Anderson (2015) there are significant associations between financial and economic strain, general stress levels, and conflict between parent and child particularly to African American males in High school setting.

In addition to physical strain, the financial stress of living in poverty takes a marked toll on the mental health and emotional well-being of youth and adolescent. Young children living in low-income neighborhoods have even been shown to be at a greater risk of developing behavioral problems (Harris, Fox & Holtz, 2015). Research on the emotional reactivity of children in low income households directly predict emotional and behavioral problems later in childhood and adolescence (Shapero & Steinberg, 2013). The impact of household chaos on adolescent mental health then depends on the child's emotional reactivity in childhood, with higher emotional reactivity associated with more emotional problems (Shapero & Steinberg, 2013).

Perry, Tabb, and Mendenhall (2015) showed that African American males that lived in neighborhoods with high rates of crime, poverty, unemployment, and violence showed a higher likelihood of developing anxiety, aggression, PTSD, and depression due to feelings of constant threat, and loss of personal control. In the case of urban neighborhoods and those with a lower percentage of African American families, African American youth experienced instability in maintaining relationships and networks with other people. Vulnerable populations of African American males living in high-crime, high-poverty neighborhoods also experience higher levels of internalization of feelings resulting from discrimination and marginalization which ultimately impacted academic engagement (Liu, Kertes, Bolland, Dick & Mustanski, 2016). Homelessness could also be a significant barrier to academic success, as shown in a study on neoliberal policies driving Chicago public schools which found that homeless families of color in Chicago were regularly excluded from accessing high-performing schools in the area (Aviles & Heybach, 2017).

Social influences

In their research study, Conchas, Lin, Oseguera & Drake (2014), social influences play a role in schools and communities thus contributes to the perception that African American males have academic and income opportunities without considering their experiences and challenges to advancement. Lack of safety within communities was shown to be a barrier to educational success (Vega, Moore III & Miranda, 2015). Low-income, impoverished, and densely populated urban African American communities and youth experience high rates of crime, delinquency, and likelihood of victimization to gang and police violence disproportionately to other demographics, such that homicide is the leading cause of death for African American male adolescents (Richardson, Van Brakle & St. Vil, 2014). Being male was identified as a factor in African American adolescent drug use, especially if they also were an older adolescent, spent time with their friends rather than family members, had friends who used drugs, and were planning to enter the military after high school; conversely, African American male adolescents were less likely to use drugs if they spent time with their family, had parents who talked to them about the dangers of drug use, were involved in extracurriculars, and had plans to attend college or post-secondary school after high school (Myers, 2013).

Poor African American families adopted many strategies to help keep youth from developing into delinquents, being incarcerated, or killed by neighborhood gang violence, crime, or police, such as family protection, child monitoring, parental resource-seeking, and in-home learning strategies (Richardson, Van Brakle & St. Vil, 2014). Temporary or permanent removal from impoverished African American communities was found to be a parenting strategy to ensure the safety of young males from inner city violence and included being sent to a relative's or family friend's house to stay or even to juvenile detention centers (Richardson, Van Brakle & St. Vil, 2014). The amount of social capital that poor families possess can be crucial in obtaining external resources to help prevent delinquency (Richardson, Van Brakle & St. Vil, 2014). Community, familial, and peer support systems and networks were shown to be critical for the college persistence of African American males (Anumba, 2015). Verbal support from family have helped to encourage students through difficult times and given them the necessary motivation to pursue and persist in higher education that is often lacking in minority communities. Academic and social support from peers and teachers in and outside the classroom were shown to enhance the success of black males in college (Anumba, 2015).

Many African American churches prioritize education and seek to help students by providing scholarships and tutoring and mentoring services (Louque & Latunde, 2014). As pillars of the African American community, black churches can also act as resources and community centers by providing prevention services and health programs for the benefit of African American community members (Weeks, Powell, Illangasekare, Rice, Wilson, Hickman & Blum, 2016). Church and African American community service organizations have especially been invested in organizing programs to uplift youth, and address urban issues, particularly to support African American boys (Savage, 2013). Black churches, African American sororities and fraternities placed education as a top priority and valued academic training and achievement, as key areas of cultural strength in African American communities. (McNair, 2013).

Louque and Latunde (2014) found that many African American families that felt excluded from participating in the school community sought out information specific to African Americans community organizations and special programs such as parent committees, tutoring programs, student alliances, and childcare resources. Parents used educational literature from libraries and the internet, as well as visits to libraries, schools, and institutional organizations such as the National Association for the Advancement of Colored People, parent/teacher associations, and the College Board to enhance their abilities to engage in children's schoolwork (Louque & Latunde, 2014). Additionally, gathering with other African American families at church and other community functions helped them gather and share information with each other (Louque & Latunde, 2014).

Despite the resources that churches provide, however, African American men tend to attend and participate in church activities less than black women, although there are programs to benefit the specific struggles that black men experience including high unemployment rate, health concerns, leadership initiatives and crime prevention (Hodges, Rowland & Isaac-Savage, 2016).

About Andrea Brown

Andrea Brown is an aspiring Doctor of Education who aims to support the students that are most often underprivileged. Andrea believes that every child and every person deserves to be given help and guidance in their own growth as students and human beings. These strong beliefs are manifested in both her professional and personal lives. Andrea has spent years volunteering at her local elementary school as a teacher's aide, collaborating with students in their achievements. In her professional experience, Andrea has founded and operated a professional cleaning service as CEO and worked in a variety of service industry management positions, where she has developed her customer service, team leadership, and accounting skills to a remarkable level. Andrea currently holds a Master of Science in Accounting from Grand Canyon University and a Bachelor of Science in Business from the University of Phoenix.

In Andrea's time working in the elementary school, she has developed encouraging and mutually rewarding relationships with both young students and experienced teachers. She frequently assisted teachers with a wide range of work, from grading papers to taking attendance to aiding children with their assignments, and even gave advice to teachers based on her perceptions of students. Her interactions with the students consisted of both caring for the children as well as challenging them to expand their areas of comfort, often acting as the extra push that a child would need to achieve more than they believed they were capable of. In order to challenge them, Andrea would break down problems into steps and questions to ask the student, as well as checking for genuine understanding of classroom material, while adapting to the individual working habits of the student. Andrea received positive feedback and constructive criticism from the teachers, which she incorporated into her work with the students in order to improve as a caretaker and guide for them.

As an entrepreneur and manager across several service industries, Andrea has demonstrated a high level of commitment to the quality of her customer service and outstanding leadership capabilities. She aims to lead by example and performs at the high standard that she expects of her team. Andrea has been commended for her top-notch service during her tenures at Sam's Club and Walmart, and has shown herself to be adept at training new employees and ensuring overall harmony within the teams that she managed.

She is committed to the long-term success of her work, as shown by the thirteen years she dedicated to patients at the Veteran Administration Hospital. Her service, leadership, and accounting skills were essential in founding her own professional cleaning service in 2007, which she currently owns and operates, and serves the greater Augusta area.

Andrea's drive to help others comes from a deep sense of empathy and compassion for those who struggle, which is bolstered by her commitment to and engagement with her church community and Christian faith. Her generosity extends to all her friends, family, and even strangers. Andrea is always the first one to lend someone a hand and offer advice, and consistently goes above and beyond what is expected of her. In this way, she hopes to make a tangible difference in the lives of children who lack the resources to achieve their fullest potential.